Original title:
Beyond the Brambles

Copyright © 2025 Creative Arts Management OÜ
All rights reserved.

Author: Evelyn Hartman
ISBN HARDBACK: 978-1-80567-311-8
ISBN PAPERBACK: 978-1-80567-610-2

Blossoms Amongst the Barbs

In a garden that's wild and not so neat,
A daisy danced with a pesky beet.
They both wore hats that were way too grand,
Claiming the title of the funniest band.

But thorns were poking at their little show,
While the roses whispered, 'You two are low!'
Yet laughter echoed through the tangled trees,
As the weeds giggled, swaying in the breeze.

The Thicket's Secret Embrace

In the thicket where the squirrels play,
A raccoon pranced in a fancy bouquet.
He tipped his hat with a flick and a grin,
Saying, 'Join the party! Let the fun begin!'

The thorns rolled their eyes, not wanting to share,
While the mushrooms chuckled, without a care.
They opened a portal with a flick and a snap,
Leading to places where all took a nap.

Treading on Twisted Roots

Oh! Watch your step on the roots that twist,
A grasshopper hops with a wide-open fist.
He challenges the beetles to a dance-off grand,
While the ants march in line, like a well-trained band.

But a snail slips by, with a trail of goo,
Saying, 'Make some room, I want to join too!'
The puddles applaud in a splashy cheer,
As the vines overhead whisper, 'Let's all draw near.'

In the Realm of Thorny Fantasies

In a land where prickers come out to play,
A cactus wore sunglasses on a sunny day.
The roses sat laughing, quite full of glee,
As a dandelion joked, 'What's thorny, not me!'

A hedgehog rolled in, spinning round and round,
Declaring, 'This thorny dance will astound!'
While the wind played a tune through the leaves overhead,

The garden burst forth with giggles instead.

The Wild's Unseen Embrace

In the woods where tangled tales hide,
A squirrel wears sneakers, who knew he'd glide?
Chasing his acorns, he slips on a vine,
Laughing at branches, they're less than benign.

The owls are gossiping, hooting with flair,
While foxes do yoga, stretching with care.
"Got any snacks?" asks the deer in the glade,
But carrots are scarce in this leafy charade.

Stories Buried Amongst the Leaves

Under the canopy, secrets abound,
Where raccoons tell stories without making a sound.
A turtle's slow waddle is met with a cheer,
As crickets all giggle and eat lots of beer.

"Hey, have you heard? The ants are in charge!
They threw a big party, it's quite the barrage!"
The trees all shake hands, their branches entwined,
While squirrels make bets on who'll stay aligned.

The Edge of Caution

When you tiptoe on brambles, hold tight to your hat,
Or you might just meet up with a comical cat.
He'll laugh at your prowess and offer his paw,
As you wrestle with weeds and recoil with awe.

The hedgehogs together are spinning a tale,
Of how they once danced without fear of the snail.
But who will remember? The thorns just don't care,
As they keep on insisting you're part of their fair.

A Whisper Amidst the Twists

In a thicket where whispers drift soft on the breeze,
A bunny debates with the wise old trees.
"Shall I dance under moonlight or nap in the ferns?"
With a wink and a shrug, he decides what he yearns.

The laughter erupts, like a bubble in stew,
As the bushes all gossip about what to do.
"Let's host a parade, with the frogs in fine shoes,
Frogs in tuxedos, oh, let's spread the news!"

The Unfurling Leaf

A leaf once curled up tight,
In sunshine found its fight.
It flapped its edges wide,
And danced with all its pride.

The breeze gave it a shove,
It twirled as if in love.
Then landed on a shoe,
Crying, "What have I done?"

It waddled off with flair,
Just like it didn't care.
"I meant to touch the sky!"
Lamented with a sigh.

A ladybug then came,
And joined in all the fame.
Together they would cause,
A ruckus, what a pause!

Breaths of the Enchanted

In a forest filled with glee,
A bunny sang with glee.
"I hop to find a snack!"
Then tumbled on its back.

The owls above would hoot,
While squirrels chased their loot.
They giggled with delight,
As shadows danced with night.

An acorn fell and rolled,
A story to be told.
"I'm not just random food!"
The acorn exclaimed, crude!

The forest laughed in jest,
Adventure is the best!
In every twist and turn,
There's giggles left to earn!

The Path Less Taken

Two paths lay side by side,
One smelled like mud and pride.
The other had a cart,
With snacks to make one start.

I chose the snacky way,
Thought I might ejeed away.
But after one big bite,
The snacks took off in flight!

I chased those sneaky chips,
With ketchup from my lips.
They giggled as they flew,
"Come catch us if you do!"

I ran with all my might,
Through bushes left and right.
But snacks can't be contained,
In the joy they've obtained!

Dreams Entwined with Nature

A flower dreamed one day,
Of becoming a bouquet.
But bees buzzed all around,
"You're lovely, dear!" they frowned.

The daisies started swaying,
While the sun kept on playing.
"Let's throw a floral dance!"
The daisies cheered, and pranced.

Their petals made a tune,
As frogs croaked in the moon.
A party spilled with cheer,
With ladybugs drawn near.

The flower twirled with glee,
As breezes set it free.
In petals bright and rare,
Life's dance was everywhere!

The Call of the Hidden Grove

In a grove where squirrels boast,
I lost my snack to a hungry ghost.
They took my chips, left me with crumbs,
Now I'm plotting my revenge with drums.

The trees they dance, oh what a sight,
Bouncing branches, just take flight!
I swear I saw a rabbit wink,
Should I ask him for a drink?

Mice hold tea parties under the moon,
Chirping crickets sing a tune.
While frogs wear crowns of dandelion,
In the kingdom of misfits, I'm relying.

So if you hear the laughter peal,
Join the fun, it's a grand ideal.
Just watch your snacks, don't trust a sprite,
In the hidden grove, all's a delight!

Navigating the Prickly Embrace

I stumbled in where thorns get chatty,
A cactus said, 'Hey, aren't you batty?'
I chuckled loud, 'You want some tea?'
But all he did was stick me with glee.

The path is wild, a twist and turn,
Where every step, I risk a burn.
The bushes gossip, oh what a scene,
A hidden world that's nothing serene.

A hedgehog rolled past, thinking he's cool,
Misguided confidence in this prickly pool.
I offered my hand, just for a shake,
He laughed and darted, made me quake!

So here I hop, with brambles to dodge,
I'll master this maze, I'm no mere lodge.
With laughter and pricks, this tale will spin,
In nature's embrace, let the fun begin!

Whispers from the Wildflower Hills

In fields where daisies have a chat,
They gossip 'bout me, the silly brat.
'Look at him bounce!' one flower gasps,
While I trip over, catching laughs in clasps.

Butterflies, too, join in the fun,
Flitting about under bright, warm sun.
I asked for advice from a buzzing bee,
He stung my toe, said, 'Dance with me!'

Every tall stem leans in close,
Telling tales of the goats they boast.
I swung my arms, in wild delight,
Spinning 'til I took off in flight!

So let's roll down this hill of blooms,
Chasing colors, making silly tunes.
In every whisper, laughter swells,
In these wildflower hills, joy compels!

A Canvas of Unruly Nature

On the canvas of weeds, oh what a blast,
Every patch painted, a ruckus amassed.
A butterfly sneezed, flew right into a pie,
Now he's stuck planning a tasty goodbye.

The daisies sprung up, in a riotous way,
Competing for who's the most fanciful display.
And I met a worm who fancied himself grand,
In a tuxedo made of the finest sand.

The clouds above wear mustache trends,
While the ants debate where the party ends.
I tried to join, but they raised a toast,
And spilled their drink, my shoes were the host!

So let's frolic in this riotous art,
With laughter and chaos, we'll never part.
In nature unbound, let spirits ignite,
A canvas of joy, what a silly sight!

Veils of Wilderness Unraveled

In a forest where squirrels play hide and seek,
A hedgehog ran off, oh what a cheek!
With a nod to the trees, he zipped left and right,
Chasing his tail, what a comical sight!

The raccoons hold meetings to scheme and to plot,
While rabbits debate on the best carrot spots.
With laughter and giggles, the forest is bright,
Who knew that the woods had such a delight?

Where Wildflowers Meet the Sky

A flower named Daisy wore a big hat,
Said, 'Watch out for bees, they might steal the chat!'
With petals like laughter that swayed in the breeze,
They danced under clouds with the utmost of ease.

Butterflies spun tales with each flit and flop,
While daisies convinced them, 'You really should stop!'
For tea with the daisies, a whimsical plan,
As insects and blooms plotted wildflower spans!

The Thicket's Silent Call

In the thicket, a chatter of critters does play,
The frogs croak their jokes, hip-hip-hooray!
With vines tangled up like a jumbled old sock,
They wait for the owl to come by and mock.

'What's down with the groundhog? Such funny old fluff!'
The badger, in jest, says, 'You can't get enough!'
While twigs snap like laughter in a breeze that's so bold,
Nature's grand humor is a sight to behold!

Dances in the Underbrush

Little ants in a line, they groove to a beat,
Swaying to rhythms of antennae and feet.
Squirrels do breakdancing, spinning around,
While hedgehogs roll by, getting dizzy on the ground.

The bushes are clapping, with leaves all a-flutter,
A wild critter party, there's no time to mutter!
With giggles and wiggles, the night becomes bright,
All critters unite for a dance under starlight!

Flora's Hidden Meanings

In the garden where secrets creep,
The daisies giggle, the roses leap.
A tulip whispers, "What's that you say?"
"I smell a salad!" the radish plays.

With carrots in hats and peas that jest,
They plot and scheme, no time for rest.
"Let's dance with the breeze!" the violets cheer,
"Or we'll end up trapped in a giant's ear!"

A Journey into the Green Unknown

In the underbrush where shadows hide,
The mushrooms gossip, with much pride.
"What's this? A fox with a funny hat!"
"It thinks it's stylish!" laughed the aristocrat.

A hedgehog waltzes, a snail sings low,
"Who needs to hurry?" they laugh and glow.
The grasshoppers hop on their concert stage,
With a jazz band made of a worm and sage!

The Realm of Entangled Wonders

In twisted vines and tangled trees,
A squirrel tells jokes, if you please.
"Why did the acorn join the band?"
"Because it had the best dance moves on land!"

The ferns bow down for the ivy queen,
While the thickets clap like a lively machine.
"Let's throw a party!" a beetle proclaims,
"Just avoid the spiders; they play funny games!"

Powers of the Whispering Willows

Under willows where giggles swirl,
A gnat's got jokes that make the world twirl.
"What's green and sings?" it buzzes with glee,
"Elvis Parsley! Come laugh with me!"

A breeze tickles leaves, they shiver with cheer,
As the wise old owl chimes, "Laughter is near!"
With branches swaying, they toast to the night,
"Here's to the humor that gives us delight!"

Tales from the Verdant Veil

In the woods where squirrels dance,
A raccoon holds a daring chance.
It swipes a snack from careless hands,
And sings its triumph in witty bands.

The owls gossip, wise and sly,
About the hare who dreams to fly.
They plot a scheme, a feathered hat,
For when he jumps and lands, splat!

A rabbit winks, with mischief bright,
In the glow of the moon's soft light.
It tells a tale of twisted vines,
Of secret paths and odd designs.

So gather 'round, the laughter swells,
In nature's realm where humor dwells.
Each critter shares a joke or pun,
In the leafy shade, they all have fun!

Finding Light in the Den

A sly little fox in the cozy nook,
Chose a pillow made of an old book.
He snickers softly, eyes all aglow,
As he dreams of a feast at the big pot of stew.

The badger who snored with a marvelous grace,
Awoke to find honey all over his face.
With sticky paws, he wobbled about,
Singing sweet songs in an excited shout.

A bear brought a cake, oh what a delight,
But dropped it on his foot in a clumsy fright.
The forest erupted in giggles and cheer,
As the bear swore he'd bake, not eat, next year!

They gathered around with cups made of pine,
Toast to their folly, their hearts all align.
Together they laughed till the stars took their place,
In the moonlit den, such a comical space!

Echoes of Nature's Secret Keepers

In the glen where whispers twine,
A squirrel teases, 'This nut is mine!'
With flips and twists, he scurries around,
Leaving the others puzzled and bound.

The turtles slow in their race of pride,
Declare a truce, and laughter's their guide.
They start a band with shells as drums,
And shake their tails to the sassy hums.

A crow with antics, sharp and spry,
Picks at the shoes of a passerby.
With a caw and a flap, he soars up high,
'Catch me if you can!' is his cheeky reply.

From shadow to light, the giggles rally,
The forest's secrets held in a caddy.
With nature's cheer, they prance and play,
In echoes of laughter, they dance the day!

Whims of the Wayward Wind

The wind waltzed in, with a cheeky sigh,
Playful and spry, it said, 'Oh my!'
It snagged the hat of a man who strolled,
And danced with delight, all cheeky and bold.

The trees swayed gently, a rustling laugh,
As leaves were tossed in a playful path.
'Let's tickle those noses!' the wind called out,
And swept through the grass with a twirl and shout.

A kite caught the breeze, soaring afar,
While a puppy chased it, 'Don't you dare spar!'
With every tug, the wind would tease,
Creating a game that made hearts please.

The sun burst forth, with its bright care,
As giggles and joy filled the air.
So let the whimsy continue to spin,
In the dance of the wind, where the fun begins!

A Light in the Tangle

In a garden where weeds like to dance,
A squirrel winks, taking a chance.
He plans a great feast, with nuts galore,
But steps on a thistle—ouch! What a chore!

Around him the mischief begins to bloom,
Rabbits are laughing, they're making a room.
With carrots and lettuce, they form a conga,
While the hedgehog just sighs, 'Oh, that's just my saga.'

A butterfly flits with a giggly swirl,
Saying, "Come join us! It's quite the whirl!"
But a goat nearby munches the charm,
"Who needs a party? I've found a new farm!"

So the tangle grows dense, full of laughter and cheer,
With the antics of critters bringing good cheer.
In this wild little patch, where fun loves to bloom,
Life rolls on sweetly, in its own wacky room.

The Untamed Journey

A hedgehog named Harold had plans for a stroll,
To explore the big world—oh what a goal!
He packed up his snacks, a few berries to munch,
But tripped on a root, oh what a big crunch!

Squirrels cackled loudly, 'Was that part of your scheme?'

But Harold just chuckled, 'It's all in the dream!'
He rolled on his back, enjoying the sun,
While ants swarmed around him, telling their pun.

The trees whispered secrets, the bushes would squeak,
As Harold made friends that were decidedly unique.
From weathered old owls to the shyest of mice,
They plotted adventures—oh, wouldn't that be nice!

A journey of laughter, where surprises unfold,
With Harold as captain, forever quite bold.
Through roots and through paths, he'd giggle and hum,
And turn every stumble into pure, silly fun!

Nature's Resilient Song

In a meadow of greens, with daisies ablaze,
A rooster sang proudly, in myriad ways.
He clucked out a tune, with much attitude,
While a snail on the ground said, "Dude, I'm not rude!"

The flowers all danced, yes, they had quite the flair,
And the bees buzzed along, with a rhythm to share.
"Let's form a parade!" chirped a chipmunk so bold,
While a tortoise muttered, "I'll catch up, if I'm told."

The wind blew a whistle, inviting them near,
As the sun beamed down with a wink and a cheer.
Together they journeyed, in laughter they thrived,
For nature's a stage where the funny survived!

And as dusk painted skies in soft shades of gold,
They sang of their stories, both silly and old.
In this wild symphony, they all played a part,
Resilient and joyful, oh, the tune of the heart!

Through the Dense and Wild

In a jungle so thick, where the laughter resounds,
A monkey named Max wore his crown of crowns.
He swung through the vines with a cheeky little grin,
While the parrots all squawked, "Let the fun now begin!"

A bear brought a picnic, a mishmash of treats,
But accidentally spilled it, oh what a feat!
The ants held a meeting, all marching in line,
"Let's seize this buffet, it's truly divine!"

The trees joined the chorus, swaying to beat,
While a badger nearby tapped his toe on his feet.
With critters in rhythm, they danced through the trees,
Twirling and whirling, all enjoying the breeze!

Through dense and through wild, the laughter was loud,
In a party of nature, they all felt so proud.
Max saluted the audience, full of delight,
In this jungle of joy, every day felt just right!

Whispers Through the Thicket

In a tangle of vines, I tripped and I fell,
Among chattering critters, all casting their spells.
A squirrel with a hat, oh what a surprise,
Told me to watch out for the dragonflies.

They giggled and squawked, those cheeky old trees,
Dancing to music played by the bees.
A worm wearing glasses offered me tea,
Said life is much better when you're fancy and free.

With branches that waved like a merry parade,
Every rustle and whisper, a joyful charade.
We laughed at the bushes that tickled my toes,
And stumbled through laughter where nobody knows.

So if you should wander where the wild things play,
Beware of the laughter that sweeps you away.
For in every thicket, there's fun to be found,
Just follow the giggles and let joy abound.

Shadows Lurk Beneath the Thorns

In the shadows beneath where the thorns like to creep,
Lies a party of shadows that never do sleep.
They dance in the dark, wearing hats made of gloom,
And tell the oddest tales under the pale moon.

A hedgehog in slippers invites you to stay,
While he jokes about snails being lazy all day.
Beware of the twigs that might stab at your feet,
They're plotting a game of hide-and-seek sweet.

Through bushes they scurry, so light on their toes,
Creatures of mischief with unmentionable woes.
A dance-off begins 'tween the owls and the mice,
But don't bring your own moves, they'll charge you a price!

So tiptoe through shadows, be careful, don't trip,
As laughter echoes softly from every nook's grip.
For lurking in thorns, in whispers and sighs,
Are stories of pranks, with mischievous lies.

A Path Through Perilous Green

I took a bold step on a whimsical path,
Where ferns tell jokes and the grass loves to laugh.
With ivy for company, weaving tales of delight,
I stumbled on a turtle who danced through the night.

An old crow named Clyde sported a fancy red tie,
Said, "Life is much funner if you give it a try!"
He juggled some acorns while singing a tune,
And twirled in a whirl, by the light of the moon.

A mischievous breeze tickled all that it caught,
Lifting leaves high for the umpteenth good-naught.
I chased after giggles that rolled like a stream,
Each bump and each tumble, just part of the dream.

Now I wander this path with a skip and a shout,
Where every mishap is what life's about.
So join in the frolic through jungles of green,
And find the delights that are seldom unseen.

Secrets of the Hidden Grove

In the grove, all is lively, full of bright tunes,
The mushrooms are chatting, discussing the moons.
Each secret's a giggle, each whisper a tease,
As rabbits in bowties discuss how to sneeze!

There's a sign that says 'Caution: Beware of the grins,'
For the faces on trees love to pull silly fins.
A badger with glasses reads stories at night,
While hedgehogs and foxes engage in a fight.

Along comes a gopher, he's bringing the snacks,
With berries and honey—who cares about facts?
They feasted on laughter as day turned to gloom,
In a dance with the shadows that brightened the room.

So if you should wander, remember this phrase,
The grove holds the secrets and jovial ways.
Just dive into fun, where the wild creatures play,
And leave all your worries to drift far away.

Trails of Forgotten Footsteps

I stumbled upon a path so wide,
Where squirrels chattered, full of pride.
Chasing shadows, I tripped and fell,
My shoes, they whispered, "Can't you tell?"

Mud splattered high and grass up my nose,
I marched like a duck in too-tight clothes.
A rabbit giggled, quick on his feet,
As I danced a jig, oh so incomplete!

The trees were laughing behind their bark,
As I clumsily strolled through the park.
Who knew that nature could be so sly?
I'm just a lost soul beneath the sky!

But every stumble is a tale to tell,
In this bumpy adventure, I weave my spell.
With each little blunder, I find my cheer,
In the trails of laughter, I'll always steer!

Where Petals Kiss the Ferns

In a field of colors, a bee went 'buzz,'
Chasing petals, without a fuss.
He crashed into a dandelion puff,
I laughed so hard, I'd had enough!

The flowers whispered secrets, loud and clear,
A snail remarked, "Do we even care?"
The fern waved back with a leafy grin,
"Join the parade; let the fun begin!"

A butterfly flapped with dramatic flair,
While I tripped over roots, a real hotshot there!
I dotted the landscape, a colorful mess,
Dancing with daisies, oh, what a dress!

So if you find joy in a moment's chance,
Just remember to join in the dance.
For where petals meet the whimsical ferns,
Laughter is treasure, and that's what we yearn!

Concealed Beauty in the Wilderness

In shadowed corners where the wild things play,
I stumbled across a hedgehog's ballet.
He twirled and he swirled, but fell on his face,
"Don't mind me," he said, "I'm just saving grace!"

The mushrooms were giggling, a curious sight,
As I tried to tiptoe; my shoes were too tight.
With every loud squish, I drew eyes around,
Could it be me, the star I had found?

A wise old owl perched, looked down with glee,
"Your style, my friend, is a sight to see!"
I waved my arms like a crazy cartoon,
For in this chaos, we all are immune!

So cherish the laughter, the twists and the quirks,
In the wilderness where humor works.
For beauty shines brightest when we lose our way,
And a little mischief makes for a grand play!

Twilight in the Twisted Grove

Twilight whispers through an oak so wide,
I saw a fox with a mischievous stride.
He winked and he danced, avoiding a smear,
While I fought off shadows that danced with fear.

The fireflies wobbled, like lights on the run,
While I fumbled and tumbled, blaming the fun.
"Who needs a flashlight when you can just trip?"
The fox laughed aloud, as I took a slip!

The trees wrapped their branches around me, oh dear!
A tumble of laughter, my heart held cheer.
As darkness descended like a big fluffy quilt,
We swayed with the winds, near the shadows we built.

So if you should wander when twilight's not shy,
Remember to giggle, to stumble and fly.
In the twisted grove, with humor in play,
Every shadow just wants to dance and sway!

Leafy Chronicles of the Solitary

A squirrel raced up the tree,
Chasing thoughts of yesterday's spree.
His acorn stash, a treasure so grand,
Turned out to be just a rubber band.

The birds all laughed at his mistake,
As he plotted more snacks for his break.
But with each scamper, he found his way,
To places where shadows and sunlight play.

The winds whispered secrets so sly,
While he pondered on how to fly high.
Yet tripping over roots was his fate,
As he chased a butterfly he called mate.

In the solitude, he wore a grin,
For the laughter of nature was deep within.
With friends like these, who needed the crowd?
Life's quirks and giggles, vibrant and loud.

The Lure of the Entwined Trails

Two rabbits hopped through the twisting vines,
Arguing over who'd win the fines.
One claimed speed, the other wit,
Together they tangled, not giving a split.

A hedgehog watched, bemused from a nook,
As the two formed a plan from a storybook.
Maybe if they ran in a zigzag's delight,
They'd confuse the fox and take flight at night.

Under leaves, they'd plotted their daring race,
But tripped over roots in their haste to chase.
With squeals of laughter, they rolled down the hill,
While the world around stood still, just a thrill.

Through the shouts and snickers of critters nearby,
They learned that competition's just lullabies.
In the thrills of the chase, they found pure gold,
For friendship's laughter never grows old.

Radiance Amidst the Shadows

In the twilight where shadows reside,
A glowworm danced with quirky pride.
His bright green light twinkled and flashed,
While grumpy frogs croaked, thoroughly bashed.

"Why shine so bright?" a wise owl said,
"Your glow just wakes all who want bed."
But the glowworm giggled, not feeling shy,
"I light up the night; I'm the star in the sky!"

In moonlit glades, they all came to see,
Beetles and critters joined in with glee.
With each little flicker, the darkness was charmed,
And the timid old owl found himself disarmed.

So under the stars, they danced 'til dawn,
In the heart of the night, every fear was gone.
Laughter echoed through the shimmering glades,
A reminder that joy is what never fades.

Journeying Through Twisted Dreams

A hedgehog set off on a journey of dreams,
With thoughts of adventure flowing like streams.
He wore a tiny hat, mismatched and bold,
And imagined brave tales that should be told.

Through twisting paths with brambles to dodge,
He stumbled upon a party at a fogged-up lodge.
Where mice strummed banjos and badgers did dance,
He couldn't help joining the fun and romance.

But mid-swirling tunes, he stepped on a shoelace,
And tumbled right down, a spiky disgrace.
The laughter erupted, a chorus so sweet,
As he twirled on the floor, with two left feet.

In the end, he stood up with a flourish and cheer,
Declaring, "I'll travel more, never fear!"
For in every blunder lies laughter to find,
And adventures await the goofy and kind.

Paths of the Untrodden

There's a trail where squirrels yell,
And bushes hold secrets, oh so swell.
A tangle of vines, what a sight,
With frogs wearing hats, what a delight!

Bumblebees buzzing their happy tune,
While rabbits dance under the moon.
Streams that giggle and rocks that sigh,
What a goofy place, oh my, oh my!

A hedgehog juggles, the crowd will cheer,
As ants play poker with their own beer.
Each path is wacky, with tales to tell,
Leading to laughter, oh so well!

The unexplored makes the wild hearts race,
Where clowns of nature join the chase.
So grab your gear, don't be forlorn,
For joy is waiting, all over worn!

Fluttering Hues of the Forgotten

In the meadow where memories itch,
Butterflies gab, oh what a glitch.
Dandelions whisper, secrets fly,
While worms in tuxedos wave goodbye!

The light is silly, winking bright,
As grasshoppers hop, full of sheer fright.
A painter's palette spills on the ground,
With colors so loud, they dance around!

The daisies giggle in lines so neat,
As clover plays tricks on your feet.
A flutter of hues, what a scene,
In the land of the giggles, wild and green!

So prance through the past, wear a grin,
For every old leaf can now begin.
The fluttering shades invite the fun,
As laughter rings 'til the day is done!

Traces of the Sunlit Refuge

In the sunny nook where shadows hide,
A raccoon puts on a dinner slide.
There's laughter echoing off the trees,
As squirrels debate, 'Who stole my cheese?'

Sunlight spills onto a patch of grass,
Where turtles race, oh what a class!
The frogs sit watching, wearing crowns,
While gophers giggle, tumbling down!

Mushrooms throw a party, quite absurd,
With snails as guests, spreading the word.
Each tickle of sun brings joy to the jest,
In this refuge, where laughter's the quest!

So follow the sun to this merry spree,
Where everything laughs, even the bee.
Come one, come all, to the light's embrace,
In the chuckles of nature, find your place!

The Heart of the Hidden Glades

In glades where mischief loves to play,
A fox wears spectacles, leading the way.
Trees whisper secrets in giggly tones,
As mushrooms dance on their little stones.

The air is full of a prankster's cheer,
With otters making a splash near here.
The ferns will sway, playing peek-a-boo,
While tigers in stripes wear pajamas too!

A otter on skates zooms past a snail,
While owls hoot nonsense, telling a tale.
It's a world where laughter makes its stand,
In the heart of the glades, come understand!

So leave behind worries, take a chance,
Join in the frolic, come join the dance.
In this hidden haven, let silliness reign,
For the heart of the woods is joy in the rain!

Odes to the Unseen Trail

Amidst the bushes, so thick and brash,
A squirrel's high jump, an acrobat's splash.
The path is hidden, we trip and we laugh,
Chasing our dreams on a winding giraffe.

Branches above swing like disco lights,
As birds play tag in their feathered flights.
We weave through thickets, unsure where to go,
Stepping on twigs like a tap-dancing show.

Lost in the woods, we create our own rules,
Skipping past hedgehogs, these nature-made stools.
The mapping is fuzzy, but laughter's our guide,
In our jumbled adventure, we take it in stride.

Murmurs from the Leafy Depths

In the thick of the green, where whispers do flow,
A fox with a hat is the star of the show.
His antics are grand, with flair and finesse,
He sings catchy tunes, causing nature to bless.

Beneath the foliage, where giggles reside,
Bunnies bounce loudly, their laughter can't hide.
A snail tells a tale, a slow-motion spree,
While critters join in for a woodland jubilee.

The mushrooms are trumpets, the leaves are enrapt,
Where shadows are jokes and the sun is a nap.
Here in this realm, absurdity reigns,
In the leafy depths, we dance in the rains.

Beneath the Wild's Embrace

Hiding from prickers, we stumble and roll,
The ground is a trampoline, giving us soul.
A raccoon in glasses reads an old book,
While wild tales spiral through each little nook.

The trees shake with laughter, they wiggle and sway,
As we trip and fall in our giddy ballet.
With every odd turn, we spot something new,
Like a picnic of ants, hosting their barbecue.

In this quirky patch, every twist is a glee,
Nature's own circus invites you to see.
So take off your shoes, let your troubles all rest,
In the wild's embrace, be absurdly blessed.

The Mysterious Aglow

In the twilight hush, with shadows that play,
A glow-worm parade leads the frogs on their way.
With twinkling lights, they form curious rows,
As fireflies giggle, sharing rumors that glow.

The bushes erupt with unexpected jest,
A hedgehog in panto, naturally dressed.
Mice munch at their cheese, holding court without fuss,
While owls hoot in jest, causing quite a ruckus.

Mysteries unfold with each chuckle we find,
As critters connive, we're humorously blind.
Under this canopy, fun sprouts like wild,
A party for all, both the gentle and wild.

The Tangle of Forgotten Dreams

In a garden overgrown with weeds,
Grew a carrot that had dreams of speed.
It wanted to race the nearest snail,
But tripped on roots and started to wail.

A dandelion danced, quite out of tune,
Wishing to play a trumpet like a loon.
It puffed its seeds with all its might,
But blew away and vanished from sight.

The tomatoes held a gossip so juicy,
About the cucumber, who felt quite choosy.
They chuckled as he donned a fine hat,
Ready to impress a flirty old rat.

In this mishmash of green and brown,
Life's funny moments can flip a frown.
Amid the chaos, dreams may seem odd,
But joy's just a tumble away from the sod.

Echoes of the Woodland Heart

In a forest thick with silly tales,
The squirrels plotted grand heist trails.
They stole acorns, their favorite snack,
But returned to find they'd lost the pack.

A wise old owl hooted with glee,
As a raccoon got stuck in a tree.
He tried to escape, oh what a sight,
But ended up snoring deep into the night.

Frogs croaked songs about their lost shoes,
Hoping the moon would share some clues.
With every hop, they found only muck,
And yet, each leap brought them more luck.

In the woodland, laughter fills the air,
Like whispers of leaves stirred without care.
From squirrel to frog, all seem to play,
The echoes of mirth chase blues away.

Beneath the Scratches of the Past

There once was a cat with a hairball spree,
Who sang to the moon, how silly, you'll see.
It spat out a tune that scared off the bats,
While plotting how to seduce some fine rats.

A raccoon, dressed fine in a shiny old vest,
Thought he looked dapper, he thought he was best.
He pranced through the junk, singing all night,
But slipped on a banana peel, what a sight!

The owls chuckled from their tree-side perch,
At the antics below, a comical search.
With feathers ruffled from laughing so hard,
They dubbed this gathering a wild backyard.

Beneath scratches of time where whimsy lies,
Life's little moments bring giggles and sighs.
From jesters in trees to mice with flair,
The past may be scratched, but we laugh everywhere.

Journey Through the Bramble's Edge

Along the path where thorns intertwine,
A hedgehog set out, looking quite fine.
With a map that was drawn by a clumsy goat,
He sighed, as he stumbled and tripped on a mote.

A beaver was busy building a dam,
With twigs and twine, he called it a jam.
He claimed that his house would win 'Home of the Year,'
Until it all fell apart, oh dear, oh dear!

A fox joined the troupe, quite full of sass,
With stories of foes and of fabulous class.
He slipped on some brambles with an elegant flip,
Proud of his tales, it turned into a trip.

Through tangled ways, they all found delight,
In missteps and laughter that brightened the night.
The journey was fun, with friends by their side,
In the wild bramble's edge, they took it with pride.

Wandering the Wildflower Maze

In a garden of laughter, I roam,
Wildflowers giggle, they feel like home.
Bees wear their buzz like a cheerful tune,
I dance in the sunshine, a joyful cartoon.

Petals are whispers that tickle my nose,
With each little step, a new story grows.
I trip on a root, but oh what a sight!
The daisies all snicker, what a pure delight!

Butterflies wink as I waddle by,
Like feelers of joy, they flutter and fly.
My hat's blown away, oh where did it go?
Nature's a jester, putting on quite a show!

In this playful circus of colors and light,
I'll wander forever, it feels so right.
The wildflower maze, a comic affair,
Where laughter blooms freely, and joy fills the air.

A Song of Thorns and Blooms

In the thick of the thicket, where roses do fight,
Thorns wear a crown, but they're not too polite.
I tango with petals, a dance so absurd,
But oh, those sharp pricks can be quite the deterred.

Sunlight shines down on this prickly parade,
With giggles and burbles, the flowers invade.
A dandelion drops the best jokes of the day,
While violets roll over in humorous play.

I tried to smell roses, oh what a mistake,
The thorny defenders soon made my heart ache.
Yet laughter arose from my thistleful plight,
With each poke and jab, I'd just chuckle with might.

So here's to the blooms where the thorns tend to tease,
Life's a bright riddle; let laughter appease.
In this garden of giggles, we bloom and we grin,
For each prick in our side, a new chuckle begins.

Secrets Lurking in the Green

Hidden away in the emerald shade,
Squirrels gossip, their secrets displayed.
A hedgehog snickers while tripping on leaves,
With whispers of mischief that no one believes.

The ferns tell tales of the deer with big dreams,
As chipmunks plot schemes at the edge of the streams.
I walked through the laughter, got caught in a net,
Fallen down giggling, now that's quite the duet!

Caterpillars fear that their coziness fades,
While ants march in rhythm, with tiny parades.
A patch of green jesters wear hats made of grass,
Each tickle of breeze brings a joke from the past.

In the shroud of the woods, where the funny things hide,
Nature's a riddle, a humorous guide.
With each rustle and giggle, a mystery appears,
Let laughter sprout freely, dispelling our fears.

The Thicket's Silent Call

In the thicket where whispers play tag,
A rabbit wears pants made of a bright happy flag.
It jumps with a jiggle, a comical sight,
While crickets join in, 'til the dark takes flight.

Trees bend in laughter, old oaks crack a grin,
The bushes erupt as the fun doth begin.
Frogs burst into song, oh what a grand croak,
With every loud leap, they just jabber and poke.

I stumbled upon a snail with a crown,
He slithered and shimmied, never wore a frown.
"Hold slow, my friend," said the wise little snail,
"To rush through the thicket is to miss the best trail."

Such wonders they weave in the hush of the night,
Imbuing each shadow with mischievous light.
So heed the soft murmurs of the thicket's delight,
And join in the jig, as we dance till it's bright!

Reaching Through the Wild Veil

In the thicket, a raccoon pranced,
Wearing a hat, oh how he danced!
Branches tangled in his haste,
For a snack, there's no time to waste!

A squirrel giggled from a nearby tree,
"Is that a raccoon, or a sight to see?"
With nuts in his paws, he started to tease,
"Your dance moves could bring anyone to their knees!"

Tangled twigs all in a row,
"Watch out!" cries the crow, "for that slippery throw!"
Raccoon stumbled, tripped on his foot,
While the squirrel laughed, "Now that's cute!"

Then came the fox, with a sly little grin,
"I hear a party, let me jump in!"
With a wink and a nod, he danced to the beat,
Nature's wild soirée, a hilarious feat!

Invincible Thread of the Wilderness

A fearless hare hopped, chasing the sun,
With thoughts of mischief and plenty of fun.
In a web of wildflowers, he took a spin,
"Catch me if you can!" he shouted with a grin.

A wise old tortoise came plodding through,
"Now what's all this ruckus about, who knew?"
But the hare just giggled and zipped on away,
Into the bushes where the butterflies play.

"Slow and steady, let's start the chase,"
The tortoise chuckled, conceding the race.
Through dandelions and thorns, they both sped,
"Who needs a path?" the hare wildly said.

Bursting through thickets, they'll laugh 'til it's dark,
In the dance of the wild, there's always a spark.
When nature's the host of a raucous affair,
Even the timid will wiggle with flair!

Nature's Curious Puzzles

In a meadow of riddles, the frogs play a game,
"Can you find me?" they croak, "it's never the same!"
Behind every leaf, a chuckle does peek,
"Is it spring or summer? It's hard to critique!"

A wise little owl wore spectacles tight,
"Is that a game piece? No, it's just a flight!"
With feathers askew and a laugh like a breeze,
He spread silly wisdom while hiding with ease.

"Why's the bee buzzing? It's not for a fight,"
"Or maybe," said the cricket, "just to feel light."
Together they capered through sunshine and shade,
In laughter, the puzzles of nature were laid.

With each curious question, they danced with delight,
For every odd riddle just added to sight.
In the quirks of the wild, with every surprise,
Lies the heart of a joke wrapped in nature's goodbyes!

Where the Leafy Veil Part

Where the leaves hang low, a secret unfolds,
"Is it magic?" asked a bunny, "or just tales of old?"
With a swish and a flick of their twitching little noses,
They peeked through the leaves where adventure proposes.

A parade of ants marched, in lines oh so neat,
"What's the occasion?" they cheered with their feet.
Said one with a top hat, "To bring snacks for a feast,
While the world laughs along, a curious beast!"

By a brook that gurgles, a frog played a tune,
With a bashful little glance, he croaked to the moon.
"Just a concert! Don't fret, it begins with a splash,
So come join the chorus, we'll dance in a dash!"

With the leafy veil parting, the stage now was set,
From sunlight to shadows, they all placed a bet.
In nature's own gala, where humor sings bright,
Every giggle weaves magic, a pure delight!

Nature's Points of Intersection

I tripped on a root, oh what a surprise,
My sandwich flew up, right into the skies.
A squirrel took a bite, while I stood in awe,
Claiming my lunch, with a nutty guffaw.

A deer peeked in, with a curious glance,
Wearing a crown made of twigs, what a chance!
It stomped its hoof, like a dance in the mist,
As if to say, "Hey, don't you dare resist!"

A raccoon in a hat, looking oh so dapper,
Juggled my apples, bit by bit, snap! Snap!
He winked as he tossed, with quite the flair,
Nature's circus? Yes, no need to beware!

As I laughed at the scene, I flew with delight,
A chipmunk squeaked, "It's just for tonight!"
So if you find jests in the wild and the green,
Just join in the fun, it's a regular scene!

Beyond the Nature's Embrace

I wandered too far, in a thicket so thick,
Where birds told jokes and the frogs played a trick.
A turtle raced by, or maybe it strolled,
In a slow-motion urge to find treasures untold.

The owl turned around, a wise old chap,
Gave me a wink, then fell into a nap.
Dancing fireflies joined, with sparkles so bright,
As night shimmied in, to tickle their flight.

There was laughter in leaves, rustles in grass,
A picnic of giggles from squirrels amassed.
Their acorn buffet, with antics divine,
Made me forget my lunch left behind!

With nature so spry, and humor in tow,
I thought, "What a place, where the merry winds blow!"
If you wander these trails, don't take it all straight,
For laughter and whimsy are nature's true fate!

Secrets from the Sylvan Labyrinth

In a maze full of trees, I stumbled around,
Where whispers of nature made the oddest sound.
A bubble of giggles floated past me with glee,
As a badger recited, "You ought to see me!"

The path was a joke, twisted and curled,
With bushes debating, "Who's best in this world?"
A fox chimed in, chuckling under his breath,
"I'm on a diet; now that's a fine jest!"

Mushrooms all gathered for a party and dance,
With a ladybug DJ, giving them a chance.
The butterflies twirled while fungi sang low,
An echo of mirth in the midnight glow.

"Follow your nose!" shouted a chipmunk nearby,
As he juggled my snacks with a glimmering eye.
Oh, secrets I've learned from this woodland spree,
Are best shared with friends, if they're lively like me!

The Dance of Soaring Spirits

A breeze whispered secrets through the thick, leafy leaves,

As hummingbirds whirled in their nightly reprieves.
With every flap, they tickled the air,
While squirrels performed acrobatics with flair.

The moon rolled in laughter, reflecting the scene,
As crickets orchestrated this nature-made dream.
A troupe of raccoons did the cha-cha-cha,
In borrowed old hats and a kazoos' suave.

Frogs played the trumpets with bulging delight,
While all around dances lit up the night.
Beneath the stars' twinkle, the spirits would cheer,
For nature's grand show with its jubilant sphere.

So next time you wander, let joy take its flight,
Join in with the wild, and don't miss the height!
For laughter's the rhythm that makes spirits soar,
A joyous embrace that forever will roar!

Journey Through the Thicket

In a maze of twisting vines,
I lost my sense of direction,
Chased by squirrels with tiny signs,
And a map full of rejection.

With each step, a new surprise,
A bush that whispers silly rhymes,
Jellybeans fall from the skies,
And I trip over my own times.

Bunny rabbits wearing shoes,
Conducting a parade in cheer,
While I dance to their funky blues,
Wishing I had packed some beer.

The thicket giggles in delight,
As I stumble and I giggle,
Who knew nature threw such a night?
Next time, I'll bring a wiggle.

Echoes of the Hidden Glade

In a glade where shadows play,
I heard a trumpet sound a tune,
A frog in shades, hip-hip-hooray!
He claimed to be a jammy croon.

Mice throw parties with a flair,
They serve tea that tastes like cheese,
And in this world, it's only fair,
To dance on tables made of trees.

Thorns wear hats and look quite grand,
While thistles spin in twirly skirts,
Their elegant moves, oh so unplanned,
As I clumsily dodge their spirts.

All the echoes laugh at me,
For I'm the jester of the scene,
But joy is what I feel, you see,
In the middle of this green.

Veil of the Enigmatic Woods

Here in woods with secrets deep,
Where shadows dance like a dream,
A raccoon's playing hide and seek,
Or maybe it's my brain's big scheme.

Trees poke fun with gossip glances,
Mushrooms burst with laughter spry,
While owls take part in wild prances,
As I ask the squirrels, 'Oh why?'

Tickles from the whispering breeze,
A ballet of leaves twirling down,
Nature's giggles bring me to knees,
Wearing an acorn for a crown.

But I shall wander and explore,
Through tangled paths, I'll frolic free,
These woods, like jokes, are never more,
Than punchlines hiding fun with glee.

Beneath the Canopy of Mysteries

Under leaves that swirl and twist,
I chase the shadows for some fun,
A chicken lost, did I insist,
On finding him before we run?

Owls play poker with their friends,
Frogs throw dice with comical flair,
The laughter echoes, never ends,
As I trip over roots laid bare.

Lost socks held captive by the vines,
Argue who's the better mate,
While moose, in bowties, sip on wines,
Debating why they're always late.

I giggle under the green-lit dome,
These woods have secrets in their veins,
And as I wander far from home,
I find joy in all their chains.

The Hedge's Mystical Touch

In a hedge where shadows dance,
A fox steps in with a silly prance.
He bumps a berry, a burst of juice,
And ends up looking like a lil' recluse.

A squirrel laughs from a leafy nook,
Watching the fox with a funny look.
"You're a mess!" he calls, with a cheeky grin,
As the fox tries to wipe it off his chin.

The hedgehog giggles, rolling with glee,
While the fox yelps, "This wasn't meant for me!"
He sneezes, and leaves a trail of goo,
The forest echoes, "What will you do?"

But every twist leads to another laugh,
With every berry, they split in half.
In the hedge, they dance and play,
Turning mishaps into a grand display.

Forgotten Paths of the Forest

A rabbit hops down the winding trail,
Where the trees weave stories, strange and pale.
He twitches his nose, lost in thought,
"What's that scent? Oh, I've got caught!"

He turns to see, a turtle fast,
Who's rolling down a hill, oh what a blast!
With a flip and a tumble, he can't quite stop,
And lands in the bushes with a cartoon plop.

The deer join in, with a gamesome cheer,
"Let's race, let's chase, no room for fear!"
But the path twists and turns like a playful tease,
With each step, they trip, and the laughter frees.

Old paths forgotten, filled with delight,
Adventures blossom from morning till night.
With each misstep, friendships grow strong,
In the forest of fun, they all belong.

Legends Woven in the Understory

In the underbrush, whispers take flight,
Of a worm who dreamed of taking a height.
He tied a leaf to make a balloon,
And shouted, "I'm off! See you soon!"

The ants gathered round, shaking their heads,
"Come back, oh worm, you'll scare the threads!"
But off he sails, in the air so grand,
As leaves start falling like a brown confetti band.

He floats past frogs croaking a tune,
"Is that a worm sailing? What a boon!"
With laughter and giggles, he drifts and sways,
Turning clouds of cotton into a fog on his days.

Back to the ground in a messy plop,
"I'll stick to wiggles," he said with a hop.
Legends spun from dreams far and wide,
In the underbrush where the funny things hide.

A Blossom's Fight Against the Thorn

A flower bloomed in a prickly patch,
Hoping to bloom, what a daring match.
With petals bright, she shimmied and swayed,
"I'll show those thorns, I'm not afraid!"

But the thorn chuckled, with a cheeky grin,
"You think you can outshine? Well, let's begin!"
A dance-off started, petals in a whirl,
While the thorns laughed, giving it a twirl.

They tangled together in a wobbly ballet,
Petals slipping, thorns leading the play.
"Watch where you poke!" the flower squealed tight,
And soon enough, they all took flight!

In a flurry of colors, they both fell down,
Laughing together, no sign of a frown.
A blossom and thorn, a curious pair,
Turning quarrels into a joyful affair.

Fluttering Heartbeats of the Forest

In the trees, a squirrel jumps high,
Chasing shadows, oh my, oh my!
The sun winks down with a golden grin,
While ants march on, all set to win.

A rabbit sneezes, loud as a drum,
Startling a bear, oh what a bummer!
The birds all laugh, they sing a tune,
While frogs dance under the lazy moon.

Mice throw a party with cheese on a plate,
But the cheese is gone—oh, what a fate!
The woodpecker pecks at a beat so sweet,
Tripping on roots with two left feet.

In this jolly world where the grass is bright,
Every creature knows how to delight.
With fluttering heartbeats and laughter loud,
The forest's alive, oh, it's such a crowd!

Where Echoes Roam Freely

In the valley, echoes leap and spin,
They tickle the flowers, coaxing a grin.
A wandering breeze carries chuckles around,
While mischief grows just beneath the ground.

A crow caws jokes that tumble and roll,
Making the foxes lose all control.
A turtle once raced but fell on his back,
Now he's the 'king' of the slow-motion pack.

The mushrooms gossip, one says, 'I'm grand!'
'But I'm much taller,' says one from the sand.
Together they giggle at things that seem strange,
At the silly debates they've arranged.

So here in the wild, where echoing calls,
Make laughter bloom in all the tree halls.
Every corner dances with stories and cheer,
Where echoes roam freely, nothing to fear!

Hidden Corners of Earth's Heart

In a patch of clovers, a crabapple sings,
Whispers of secrets that mischief brings.
A hedgehog rolls with a plucky little cheer,
Declaring loudly, 'The coast is clear!'

A snail sets off for a journey so wide,
But takes a wrong turn and gets lost in the tide.
He meets a wise owl, who gives him a wink,
'Just follow the mushrooms, they'll help you think!'

A patch of grass makes a cozy bed,
But ants have claimed it, as their royal thread.
They throw a parade, with a crumb for a float,
While the beetles march on, all in one coat.

The corners of Earth hide giggles so sweet,
With creatures and whispers that can't be beat.
So peek inside shadows, and don't be shy,
You'll find hidden stories that drift and fly!

The Stories Inside the Shrubs

In the thickets, chortles echo quite loud,
As the ladybugs dance, oh, they're feeling proud.
A hedgerow committee plans a great feast,
While the spiders spin tales of an uninvited beast.

A rabbit debates with a wise old gnome,
About which route makes the best journey home.
They draw up maps made of twigs and leaves,
Imagining wonders that nobody believes.

A weed pulls a prank on a flower so bright,
'You're in my spot!' shouted the flower with fright.
But the weed just chuckled, 'We share this place,'
As the garden erupted in a comical race.

So peer through the leaves, find joy in the scene,
Where stories unfold like a lively routine.
In shrubby embrace, adventures begin,
With the laughter of nature, let the fun spin!

Through the Tangle of Thorns

In a garden of prickles, I tripped on a shoe,
The thorns laughed aloud, said, "We're all here for you!"
With every sharp jab and every wild twist,
I danced through the chaos, too fun to resist.

A hedgehog appeared, sporting quite a grin,
"With you in the bramble, let mayhem begin!"
We huddled together, like peas in a pod,
As the thorns shared their secrets, both silly and odd.

With conga lines started by creatures so sly,
The bushes were bouncing, oh me, oh my!
A rabbit with flair wore a top hat so dapper,
While a ladybug led a raucous old caper.

So if you are lost in a maze made of green,
Just giggle and wiggle, join the wacky scene!
For in every scratch and each twist along,
There's laughter aplenty; let's sing a new song!

Secrets of the Hidden Path

In a thicket of secrets, where no one can snooze,
I stumbled on gossip shared by the blues.
The squirrels exchanged tales of epic nut heists,
While the foxes plotted adventures for feasts.

There's treasure in laughter, down each winding bend,
As flowers conspire while gossiping, friend.
Whispers of mischief float through the leaves,
With secrets so silly, it's hard to believe!

A butterfly fluttered, all glittery bright,
Said, "Did you hear? They've lost the moonlight!"
And the trees all chuckled, their branches a sway,
As they plotted to keep the night from the day.

So take off your boots; let adventure commence,
For hidden path secrets are all quite immense!
With giggles and grins, we dance through the wood,
In the land of the silly, everyone's good!

Embrace of the Untamed

An otter approached me, with fur all askew,
"Let's skate on the river, I'll show you my crew!"
With a splash and a giggle, we slid down the brook,
Embracing the chaos, with no time to cook.

The reeds waved their arms, cheering all around,
As frogs croaked in rhythm, a bouncy sound.
With laughter erupting from every last spot,
We danced with the wild, who cared if we fought?

A turtle in shades said, "Why move fast or stress?"
While a party of bugs brought a picnic, no less!
The feast was delightful, with cake made of grass,
Each bite was a laughter, oh how time did pass!

So if you feel tangled in life's endless game,
Remember the wild loves to giggle and tame.
In each little moment, let joy take the stage,
For in untamed merriment, we'll turn every page!

Dances Among the Twisted Roots

In the forest's embrace, old roots had their say,
"Join us for a dance, hip-hop and ballet!"
The vines all were swaying, the mushrooms gave cheer,
As we twirled and we giggled, free from all fear.

A raccoon DJ spun beats made of leaves,
While owls hooted wisdom that nobody believes.
We shuffled and jived, with a wink and a grin,
Who knew old roots had such rhythm within?

The fireflies flashed, a disco ball's sheen,
As crickets played tunes in a grand, leafy scene.
We twinkled and sparkled under starlit glow,
Dancing boldly with nature's show.

So come join the frolic, let your spirit run free,
In the company of roots, just trust and just be!
With laughter entwined, the night will not cease,
For in twisted adventures, we find only peace!

The Dance of Resilience

In the garden where weeds twirl,
A snail slips, giving life a whirl.
With a hop, the frog joins the spree,
Singing tunes of glee, oh so free.

Ladybugs waltz in a grand parade,
While bees cut in, their tunes unmade.
A rubber chicken falls from the sky,
And who knew plants like to fly?

Every thorn has a dance to share,
With laughter echoing through the air.
The grasshoppers shimmy, what a sight,
In this wild fest, all's perfectly right.

So grab your friends, come join the fun,
In this bustling patch where all is spun.
With every twirl, we truly embrace,
Life's quirks with a smile on our face.

Heartbeats in the Hedgerow

A bumblebee buzzes with flair and noise,
While caterpillars mumble about lost toys.
Rabbits gossip in their fluffy coats,
Spilling secrets on weather and oats.

A squirrel does aerobics on a branch,
While hedgehogs plan an outrageous dance.
Though brambles poke like prickly hats,
Laughter rings louder than chitchat chitchats.

The jays provide a raucous score,
As raccoons sneak in for snacks galore.
"Why did the tree fall?" the crow crows twice,
"Because it saw the humor and thought, 'How nice!'"

In this wild world, joy beats fast,
Every heartbeat's a giggle, a blast.
Nature's party, a raucous row,
Where laughter blooms, oh, don't say how!

Whispers in the Overgrowth

Behind the leaves where shadows creep,
A sloth snores loud, disturbing sleep.
"Are you awake?" the fern plants tease,
"Or dreaming of sandwiches and cheese?"

A hedgehog spills sage over tea,
While moths exchange gossip, breezy and free.
"Is it true that roses smell like socks?"
Said the rabbit, laughing at paradox rocks.

In the thicket thick, a dance floor grows,
With every step, a flower glows.
The world of green reveals its charms,
As critters prance with wiggly arms.

So come, my friend, join this lively crowd,
In whispers where laughter blooms so loud.
In the overgrowth, joy's the best art,
Nature's giggles tickle the heart.

Shadows of the Wild

In the twilight where shadows play,
A badger sneaks in a curious way.
"Why did the owl wear shoes?" it said,
"To dance with the moon instead of dread!"

Amidst the ferns, where critters hide,
A raccoon shapes his nightly ride.
With acorns as maracas in hand,
He grooves under stars and takes a stand.

The fox cracks jokes, a sly display,
As crickets hum, making sweet hay.
"Life's too short to just sit still,"
He grins wide, "Join me for the thrill!"

In shadows deep, joy takes a light,
Painting the night with laughter bright.
So wander here, where wild things sing,
In the shadows of life, let the chuckles ring.

www.ingramcontent.com/pod-product-compliance
Lightning Source LLC
Chambersburg PA
CBHW071839160426
43209CB00003B/354